Aunt Crystal & The Vowel Towels

Sandy Ryerse

Aunt Crystal Press

For my Ricky Awesome!

Copyright © 2023 by Sandy Ryerse

All rights reserved.

No portion of this book may be reproduced in any form without written permission from the publisher or author, except as permitted by copyright law.

ISBN 978-1-7387595-0-7

Aunt Crystal Press

www.sandyryerse.com

Cover design by Get Covers

Chapter One

ON THE MORNING AFTER the best birthday party ever in the whole wide world, I hugged my blankets really really tight, rolled over, and blinked crusty sleep from my eyes.

To sleep in or not sleep in? Ahhhhh, that was the question. Being eight was going to be easy-peasy.

While I decided whether to get up, I spied my Maximus Grossness Science Lab kit I got for my birthday. It sat on my desk, all oozy and gross in front of my new Commander Hawk dry-erase board.

Hey, Mom left me a note on the board.

Good morning, Punkinhead!

Remember, Aunt Crystal arrives today.

Don't forget to thank her for the gift.

Yay! One more birthday gift! Her gifts were always totally awesome!

Todd, please work on no more exaggerating.

Love, Mom

After last week's exaggeration flop (it wasn't MY fault the dog across the street looked exactly like a bear), I guessed it really was time to make a change.

A-hunka-hunka-hunka. A-hunka-hunka-hunka, sputter, sputter, hisssss. Only one car in the whole wide world made that noise. I yanked my very favorite hockey jersey - ten sizes too small - over my head and opened my bedroom curtains. I was right. Aunt Crystal's lime green 1957 VW Beetle was parked in our driveway.

Mom, Dad, and my six-year-old sister, Taryn, stampeded like a hundred buffalo to open the front door, but I waited in my room. I finished getting dressed. No sense in looking too eager for my birthday present. Aunt Crystal always brought my gift one day late. And my gift was always crazy-weird, totally unexpected, and soooooo perfect. Today it looked like I might have hit the mega jackpot because she juggled five or six bright green gift bags stuffed with tons and tons of that tissue stuff.

"I'm here!" Aunt Crystal called as she gathered her things and hip-checked the car door closed. She caught her really, really, really long, suede vest in the door. "Oh bother. At least I didn't lose my tail." Aunt Crystal laughed at herself as she tugged her vest free. "Too many buttons, too many buttons."

Sure enough, a button popped off the front of the vest and shot at least twenty-five feet across the driveway into the snow. I snickered from my bedroom window. There had to be 100 buttons on that vest. She could afford to lose a few.

"What's the word hummingbird?" Aunt Crystal stamped the snow off her knee-high, beaded, moccasin boots, and dropped all the gift bags at the front door before beginning her round of hugs.

I tiptoed to the top of the stairs like a cat burglar. Were all those gifts for me? I squatted down and peeked through the banister at the top of the stairs. My feet poked through the wooden spindles. Darn it, I was wearing mismatched socks again.

I forced myself to walk slowly down the stairs. Two days ago I would have jumped on the wooden banister and landed at her feet in a millisecond, but I was eight now. I shouldn't act like an excited seven-year-old.

"Hi." I landed on the bottom step and tried to look casual. I forced my gaze away from the gifts, but the bright bags covered with birthday symbols, sayings, and greetings kept drawing my eyes back. They were all for me.

Rustle, rustle, rustle, slushhhhhhhhh. One of the bags fell over and the tissue fell out.

"There's old blue eyes. Well, don't you look older this morning?" My aunt smirked. "You're still not too old for a squeeze."

She pulled me close. I was just tall enough to see over her shoulder. The gifts were too big to be electronics, too small to be boogie boards, and definitely the wrong shape to be books. Suddenly, a pair of crazy-looking sunglasses covered with a million silver sparkly sequins tumbled out of the fallen bag. In a blink, a tiny, grey, hairy elephant trunk snapped through the tissue like a lizard tongue and yanked the glasses back inside the bag like lightning.

"Did you see that? There's a Rubik's cube-sized elephant in the bag!" I tried to lunge for the gift.

"Todd." Mom wagged her finger and stepped in front of the bag as she gave me her no-more-exaggerating look.

"Come on in." Mom hooked her arm through Aunt Crystal's. "The coffee is brewing, and the cinnamon rolls are warm."

Taryn grabbed Aunt Crystal's other arm. "I've been wondering lately, are you really my dad's little sister? You're prettier than he is."

They dragged Aunt Crystal off to the kitchen.

"But Mom . . ." I pleaded, but I got the *don't-go-there* squiggly-lined forehead from her as she glanced back over her shoulder.

"Todd." Dad put his arm around my shoulder as we followed behind to the kitchen. "Last month, we had twelve firefighters and three fire trucks at our house because you told a 9-1-1 operator that our house was a fiery inferno when, in fact, the smoke you saw was actually just condensation from the dryer vent. The month before, we had twenty-three cases of ginger ale delivered to our home because you told Vickerman's Drugstore that's what your mother needed you to order because she was really, really, really sick. But the biggest blunder was when the SWAT team showed up at poor ol' Mrs. Weeks's house last summer after you reported a prowler, carrying a stash of guns, entering her backyard. That poor utility man nearly had a heart attack when taken down. Now, do you see why your mother and I are trying to get you to stop exaggerating?" He kissed the top of my head and squeezed my shoulder.

"Mmmmmm, I thought I smelled warm cinnamon when I walked in the door." Aunt Crystal whiffed the air as she was ushered to the kitchen table. "Where are the rest of the birthday partiers?"

"Oh, the Commander Hawk birthday party was yesterday for those in Todd's class," Mom stood with hands on her hips. "Commander Hawk was everywhere: cupcakes and balloons and streamers and masks and placemats and cups and banners and face painting, topped off with shields and gauntlets and rings and cake." Mom gasped for a big breath and pointed to the one remaining Commander Hawk streamer still taped to the ceiling fan.

"And you thought I wouldn't want to party with the Commander Hawk fans?" Aunt Crystal giggled and finished undoing her 99 buttons. She handed her winter coat-vest to Dad to hang up.

"Todd, I brought all the bags in here." Aunt Crystal's eyes twinkled like we were going to share the best secret in the whole wide world, but then she gave me the wide-eyed, don't-say-anything-right-now look. "I've numbered them so you could open them in order."

"Woohoo! What bag do I start with?" I sloshed through some of the tissue paper, looking for the little hairy elephant. I'd always wanted an elephant for a pet.

Chapter Two

"**B**AG NUMBER ONE, I'M going in." At the speed of light, I whipped out the tissue and grabbed a huge orangey-yellow . . . bath towel?

"Ah, extremely fluffy." I tried to sound happy about the gift. The towel was really, really, really bright and a whole lot of sissy. I bet she threw it in to throw me off the real gift. The elephant.

Mom's right eyebrow shot up like the fastest-growing bamboo shoot in the world. Uh oh. Was I exaggerating again? Or could she tell I was faking my happiness about getting a not-so-awesome towel for a birthday present?

"Hey, it's got a big letter **A** on it!" Taryn grabbed the towel and buried her face in it. "Aunt Crystal, Todd's name doesn't start with **A**."

"Todd, you're supposed to open the card first." Mom's eyebrow still spiked like a mile-high tent post.

Man, this being-older *thing* wasn't so easy-peasy so far. I snapped out of my disappointment and went on the hunt for the missing card. "It must be in bag number one." Nope. I lifted bag number two. "Nope, not under there. Hmmmm."

"Found it," Taryn squealed. "I caught Ezra marching off with it." She skipped in from the den, card in hand.

"Who's Ezra?" Dad poked his head in the den. His head jerked one way and then the other in search of whoever Ezra was.

"Earl's twin brother," she said very matter-of-factly and skipped right by Dad back into the den. "He's trying to be so cool wearing sunglasses, but they are waaaaay too big for his face. It's so cute how he tries to hold them on with his trunk," she yelled back over her shoulder.

There is an elephant! I knew it! But how did Taryn know his name? And how did she know he had a twin brother named Earl? And how come she didn't get in trouble for saying she saw an elephant? Hmmm. A little unfair.

I hoped the card would hold a clue, some good news, or at the very least, a hint about why Aunt Crystal gave me a towel. But the card was just a bright blue piece of cardboard. I read it out loud with my best radio voice. "**A**, **E**, **I**, **O**, **U**, and sometimes **Y**. Happy Birthday! Love, Aunt Crystal." I took a bow because my reading was totally magnificent. I crossed my fingers that gift number two was better than gift number one.

"Oh, another towel. Super-dee-duper fluffy." I fake-smiled. Aunt Crystal had lost her touch with picking out cool gifts.

"With an **E** on it, Todd." Taryn had joined the party again. "Just like the card said."

She was more into these gifts than I was.

Towel number two was totally purple and ginormously ugly. It was the same color as eggplant, that wickedly gross vegetable Mom sometimes made us eat. Yuck. I pulled out my best fake smile and grabbed bag number three.

"Let me guess, another towel. And according to your card, it should have an **I** on it, right?"

I was right.

I was confident that the next three bags would contain towels decked out with an **O**, **U**, and **Y** on them. As I opened each bag, I laughed and joked and tried to hide my disappointment.

"Did Mom tell you I get to shower now instead of taking a bath now that I'm eight?" I hugged Aunt Crystal and promised that I would use the towels.

She returned my hug and whispered in my ear, "Don't forget, **A**, **E**, **I**, **O**, **U**, and sometimes **Y**." Then she smushed my perfectly combed hair, like she always did, and then smirked.

Hmmmmm. That was an awfully strange smirk, even for Aunt Crystal.

"Toooooooooodddddd," Taryn squealed, as I lifted her high enough to stuff her into one of the big gift bags.

"Try getting out of that one." I stuffed the tissue paper into the bag around her, a little down her shirt, and some into her pockets. Taryn yelled as she teeter-tottered back and forth. She loved every minute until she fell over.

Then I spotted two wiggly trunks at the top of the stairs between the banister rungs. "See ya." I scooped up my tower of towels and ran after those sneaky elephants.

Chapter Three

On Sunday morning, I looked outside to see the beginning of a real northern winter coming fast. The light sheet of snow that had covered the grass the last few days had deepened overnight into a thick, thick, thick, thick, thick blanket of the white stuff. Sweet, but I wasn't in the mood to go outside today. Living my best life, I laid in bed like every day was a snow day!

"Good morning, Commander Hawk. 'Faithful for keeps, focus for life, and finish forevermore!'" I saluted my favorite superhero as he stared at me from my dry-erase board. I laughed. It was just Mom who wrote on the board. It wasn't really Commander Hawk. I wonder if I would have known that when I was seven.

Good morning, Punkinhead. Remember,

Don't forget to write Aunt Crystal a thank you note for her birthday gift.

Aunt Crystal's gift was the biggest bummer in the whole wide world . . . well, unless I could find those elephants!

Keep working on your exaggerating problem.

I bet if I asked a hundred thousand people, they would say I didn't exaggerate too much.

Keep your showers to five minutes.

No more baths for me! I was eight!

Have an awesome day!

Love, Mom

I rolled back over in my bed. I had a lot of birthday gifts to explore and a few books to read. Hmmm, what did I feel like doing? Shower first, breakfast second, and then I'd decide. I jumped out of bed and headed to the bathroom.

I skidded to a ten-foot-long, full sock-on-hardwood-floor stop. "Retreat." I marched back to my bedroom because I forgot to grab one of my new vowel towels. I grabbed the **A** towel and headed back to shower like eight-year-olds do.

"Don't forget, Todd," my dad yelled through the bathroom door. "We pay for the water, so keep your shower short and sweet."

"I won't forget," I yelled back. I set the timer on my Commander Hawk G-Brain watch to five minutes, dropped the towel on the floor, and jumped into the hot, steamy shower to lather up like an eight-year-old.

The smell of apples and almonds attacked my nostrils. Where did that come from? I turned the bottle of shampoo over in my hands. Aaah, *Granny Smith is Nuts* was the name of the shampoo. That explained it. I squeezed out a dime-sized dot of shampoo, like Mom told me a hundred times, and scrubbed my noggin. The hot water pounded like Niagara Falls.

Cluck, cluck, munch, munch, munch, snort, cluck.

I froze. "What was that?" I perked my ears to listen.

Very weak, itty bitty, tiny sounds of polka music played.

Nah, it couldn't be. Just ignore it. My five minutes were almost up. Press on.

Plink, plunk, plunk, plunk, plunk, plink, plunk, plunk, plunk. Cluck, cluck, munch, munch, munch, snort, cluck.

I froze again. It's nothing. I should just keep going. I only had a minute left to shower.

I shook my head, flinging water droplets everywhere. I rinsed off, stepped one foot outside the curtain to grab the **A** towel and –"Aaaaaaaaaaaaaaaaaaaaaaaaaargh!" I jumped back into the shower. I clutched the shower curtain with one hand and the soap dish with the other to steady myself. I had to catch my breath. "There is no way. It couldn't be."

I peeked out just a smidgen.

A million acorns camouflaged the entire bathroom floor. Airplanes, alligators, and alphabet letters totally covered the bathroom walls. Angora aardvarks, munching on asparagus, laid where I had left my slippers. Well, that explained the munching and clucking.

The window curtains had changed to the same yellow color as my **A** towel. I squinted to see the word *amber* was written all over them. *Amber?* The only time I'd heard of the color *amber* was when my mom nagged my dad for speeding through a yellow light. That was definitely the same orangey-yellow color as my **A** towel.

A really, really, really long line of angry army ants marched across the top of the bathroom mirror. They pointed at me, swaying and singing *America The Beautiful.* They were terrific!

Allan (his name was appliquéd on the front of his apron), a kind-looking artist, stood on the vanity countertop with his hand over his heart and swayed along to the musical ants. He wiped a tear and began to adjust the alarm clock in his left hand. He groaned as he bent over to rub his achy ankles with one of the paint brushes sticking out of his pockets. That's when he noticed me. He drew an arrow like a sword out of his afro, aimed it at me, and apologized for how aggressively he had been playing the accordion. So he was to blame for the polka music.

"Apologies, Todd, apologies," he repeated with an Australian accent.

FBI agent, Alex (it said so on his badge), tapped me on my shoulder and adjusted the shower curtain.

"Aaaaah! You scared me to death!" I wrapped the shower curtain around me a little tighter.

He ate a bowl of applesauce and waved four cards at me. "Aces, Todd, all aces."

I bumped Alex away from the shower curtain with my shoulder. "Get away from me!"

Then I heard, "Four plus four minus six times twenty divided by seven is . . . oh, I think I need help." On the back of the bathroom door hung an angel calculating arithmetic on his fingers. He pointed at me. "Did you bring your abacus?"

I shook my head *no*.

I yanked the shower curtain shut. I tapped my temples really, really, really fast. What to do, what to do? Think, think, think. What would an eight-year-old do in this situation? I could handle this, I told myself. I held my breath for courage. I straightened up, pulled my shoulders back, and announced, "I am coming out now."

With my **A** towel wrapped tightly around my waist, I whipped back the shower curtain and—they were all gone! Everyone and everything. Gone. Alligators and airplanes gone. Alex, Allan, ants, acorns, and angel — all gone. I dragged my hand across my forehead. I must be coming down with something.

I turned on the sink faucet, brushed my teeth, and gelled my hair. I searched for any sign of the world that had just happened. Did it really happen? Was I seeing things? Where did they go? Aha, I could still smell the apple and almond. But wait. That was the shampoo.

I twisted the doorknob to leave, but out of the corner of my eye, I saw something. Letters mysteriously appeared on the steamy bathroom mirror. *A, E, I, O, U, and sometimes Y.*

Oh boy, I needed to talk to Aunt Crystal.

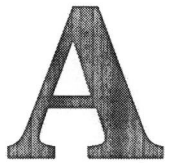

Chapter Four

I WOKE UP ON Monday morning with a million knots in my stomach, but I saluted Commander Hawk and tried to be positive. "Faithful for keeps, focus for life, and finish forevermore! I can't wait till your new movie comes out next week. Eric, Deshaun, Chad, and I are going to be first in line!"

I checked my mom's notes on the Commander Hawk dry-erase board.

Happy Monday, Punkinhead:

Thank you for keeping your shower short and sweet.

My parents would think something was weird if I didn't have a shower today. I had made such a big deal about turning eight and being able to shower. But now my belly flip-flopped about using the next vowel towel.

Keep working on your exaggerating problem.

If I told anyone about yesterday, they would just think I was exaggerating again.

Have an amazing day.

Love, Mom!

Being eight was super hard so far.

With the second towel stuffed under my arm, I marched to the bathroom, but my legs wobbled like mushy, jiggly jelly. I can do this. I can do this, I told myself. I clutched the extremely ugly eggplant-colored towel and flung open the bathroom door. And then backed out and slammed the door shut as an elk on an exercise bike, enjoying a glass of eggnog, snapped elastics at me. *It* didn't even wait until I was in the shower. Whatever *it* was. Someone or something slipped an envelope under the door out into the hallway. Written on the front, in eyeliner, was a note that said *Exit now*! The back was sealed with a scary, eerie emoji sticker. I ripped it open. Nothing inside. That's just weird.

I paced the hallway. What would be worse? Explaining *this* to my family or going in there? Should I go in? I could just walk away and let someone else deal with *it*. Maybe *it* would just disappear. Maybe I'm seeing things. Maybe I could tell Mom and Dad that I could go back to taking a bath or showering once a week or once a year. I had to think this through.

I took a double take, a triple take, and then a quadruple take up and down the hallway. No one. I knelt down on my knees like a super sleuth and cracked open the bathroom door to do surveillance. Commander Hawk would have been proud of me.

As I peeked inside, Elvis, lounging on an easy chair, flipped up the collar of his elaborate emerald-green jumpsuit and sang, "Egg rolls, egg rolls in my hand, take me to the elderberry land," over and over and over again.

Elton peered at me over the top of the wild sunglasses he was wearing, last seen on Ezra. He sat on an ebony piano bench with his elbows perched on the edge of the bathtub part of the shower.

"Enter, Todd." Elton waved me in. With his finest English accent, he announced, "It's feeding time."

Over his shoulder, I could see that the shower curtain was now the totally gross color of my towel. In the far corner where our linen closet used to be, two emus embraced in an elevator.

Wow, I wasn't sure how I felt about an elevator in our bathroom.

Elvis and Elton fed Easter eggs to eight tiny elephants wearing earrings etched with their names; Edith, Earl, Edmund, Erica, Emma, Edna, Evan, and Ezra. That's how Taryn knew their names! Each energetically exercised their ears. Ezra batted his eyelashes, all sweet and innocent. Yeah, right.

"Enter at your own risk, Todd," the emu with the excessive elbows suggested. He pointed to the far corner.

I cranked my head to see that the Eiffel Tower now stood where our toilet used to be. An Egyptian flag waved from the top. Strange. I thought the Eiffel Tower was from France. The strong smell of eucalyptus stung my nose.

"Hey, stop that!" I snapped at Earl and Ezra and ducked behind an enormous can of evaporated milk as they hurled warm Easter eggs at me.

Splat, splat, splat. What a mess!

Two eagles perched on the ceiling fan, eagerly reading the **E** encyclopedia, stopped to encourage Earl and Ezra.

"Hit him high," snickered one.

"Hit him low," giggled the other.

"Just hit him." They flapped their enormous wings and laughed in unison.

I dove into the hallway and slammed the door. Thud, thud, thud! More eggs hit the back of the door.

I wasn't ready to explain *this* to my family. Whatever *this* was. I cracked the door open a teeny, weeny, itty bit, but before I could figure out how to get rid of them, they were gone. Everything was gone. I opened the door wide. There was absolutely no sign of anything **E** except for the towel hanging over my shoulder.

"Good morning." Dad leaned over my shoulder and grinned ear-to-ear. "Are you done in the bathroom?"

I jumped seventeen feet in the air. "Uh," is all that came out of my mouth.

"Are you okay?" He lifted my chin and looked directly into my eyes.

"Yeah, I'm okay. Just heading in for my shower." I scrambled into the bathroom before Dad asked any more questions. My brain spun like a killer ping-pong ball. I looked in every crack and corner of the bathroom for the **E** things, but there was no sign of them anywhere.

After a very quiet breakfast, I left for school.

Tap, tap, tap.

I stopped at the end of our driveway and looked up in the direction of the tapping. Earl and Ezra rapped on my bedroom window and pointed with their hairy trunks. They laughed like crazy. They laughed so hard that Ezra rolled over on his back and fell off the window sill.

Served him right.

Earl snorted so hard that chocolate Easter eggs spewed out of his trunk. Great. Now I had that mess to clean up when I got home.

Should I tell anyone? I couldn't even call Aunt Crystal because she was out of town until Saturday. She had to know about this. Was that why she smirked? What was her message *A, E, I, O, U, and sometimes Y*, all about? Why do I need to know this?

Oh, so many questions.

Chapter Five

"Not-so-good morning, Commander Hawk. Faithful for keeps, focus for life, and finish forevermore." I saluted half-heartedly as I woke up Tuesday morning. "Oh, and Commander Hawk, turning eight pretty well stinks." Then I read on to see what Mom had to say for today.

It's Tuesday, Todd!

Don't forget to wear your hat and mitts. It's very cold today.

Please remember to hang up your towel on the back of your bedroom door after you shower.

If I couldn't talk to Aunt Crystal about these towels soon, I think I would burst into a katrillion pieces.

Keep working on not exaggerating.

There was no way in the whole wide world that I exaggerated as much as everyone says. If I did, I would work at never, ever, ever, ever exaggerating again.

You have basketball practice after school today.

Love, Mom!

I wanted to tell the guys about the vowel towels, but they would think I was making it up. These towels made me wonder if I was crazy. Being eight was really, really, really hard.

I headed to the shower on Tuesday morning, clutching my towel. "Ok, fluffy kind-of-white towel," I stroked the embroidered **I**. "Let's see what you can do." Something dropped out of the towel. It was the blue sort-of birthday card from Aunt Crystal. *A, E, I, O, U and sometimes Y. Happy Birthday, Love Aunt Crystal.* "Hummmmmph, this is the quackadoodliest gift ever." I scooped it up and headed to the bathroom.

I rattled the bathroom door handle. It was locked tighter than a fat gerbil stuck in a toilet paper tube. Uh oh, Dad was in there. I could hear him humming. Would the vowel world appear to Dad? How would I explain it? How . . .

"Good morning," Dad sang as he exited the bathroom and slid by me in the hallway.

Dad was always so super chipper in the morning.

"The shower is all yours. Remember, we pay for the water, so keep it short and sweet."

"Thanks, Dad. I haven't been taking too long." I looked down at his feet. He always wears the insane-est socks with his suit.

I peeked into the steamy bathroom. I inhaled big, walked through the door, and waited. I waited and waited. Nothing. I waited some more. The room looked exactly like it had looked for the past eight years — at least as long as I could remember. Aha. *It* might happen while I was in the shower, just like *it* did on Sunday. I prepared for the post-shower circus and yanked back the curtain to get in.

"AAAAAAAAHHHHHH!" I dove for my towel.

Creepy crawly vines of green ivy filled the shower. They inched toward me, ready to attack. I cowered in the corner.

They weaved around my toes, heels, and calves of my legs. Ugh. Slimy. I grabbed at them and tried to tear off the winding beasts.

I peered through the jungle of leaves to see a gang of injured insects curled up in the soap dish. They wore bandages, casts, and crutches. But that didn't stop them from impatiently eating Italian ice cream cones and drinking iced tea. The crunch, crunch, crunch of the cones, and the itty-bitty clinking of the glass increased as the bugs cheered with their mugs.

Infrared lights bounced all over the room. That made it hard to see the tiny ice-dancing instructor perched on the shower head. She juggled clothes irons by their cords. One swooshed by my head.

"Hey, watch it," I snapped.

A huge bottle of ink wobbled on top of her head. It teetered a little to the left and then a lot to the right. Dots of ink splattered all over my face and arms and covered me in blue freckles.

Incredibly, three life-sized impersonators crawled out from behind the ivy. They wore ivory-colored sweaters, the same color as my towel. They interlocked arms and stepped right by me.

Isla Fisher ignored me. Indiana Jones imitated how Isla shuffled. And Ivan the Terrible intercepted an iron headed for me. They sat down on three massively gigantic heads of iceberg lettuce and invented interesting names for infants.

"Izzy the Incredible." Isla crossed her arms across her chest pleased with her suggestion.

"Igor the Idiot," Ivan piped up.

"Not for a child," Indiana interjected. "How about Irish Ingrid or Itchy Ian?"

They grew louder and louder. My face was getting warm and my ears were popping inside. I was afraid that the impersonators might stomp out of the bathroom if their conversation got any hotter.

I jumped up with the ivy still strangling my ankles and blocked the door.

Then, to my left, I noticed an iguana burning incense in the sink. It stunk like rotten irises. His tongue snapped at my elbow, licking off some of the ink.

"Honey, are you almost done? I need to shower this morning, too." My mother's muffled words came through the bathroom door.

I gulped as big as a whale chugging the seven seas. "I'll be out soon, Mom."

I immediately interrupted the impersonators. "Shush. You gotta go back to where you came from." I turned the tap on to snuff out the incense. I tucked the iguana into Indiana's satchel then inched the impersonators back toward the shower.

Isla turned and handed me the little blue birthday card.

"Hey, where did you get that?" I grabbed the card and pushed the impersonators into the shower with all my might.

Ivan winked, "Don't forget, *A, E, I, O, U, and sometimes Y.*" And then they all snickered.

"I won't. I won't!" I yanked the shower curtain closed behind them, shut my eyes, inhaled big, and turned on the icy cold water.

"I believe, I believe, I believe," I repeated, wishing that the **I** characters would be gone.

I peeked behind the curtain. Now a billion tiny little igloos filled the shower. Being from the north, I knew exactly what would get rid of igloos. I blasted them with hot, steamy water. Yep, they were all gone. So I jumped in for my shower.

When I finished, there was no sign of any leftover **I** items for my mother to see when I left the bathroom.

"There you go, Mom. Sorry, I took longer than usual." I ran to my room before questions popped into her mind.

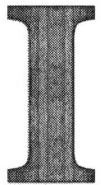

Chapter Six

I WAS STILL BIG-TIME bugged about the circus of **I** letters from this morning's shower, and hugely nervous that I hadn't seen Ezra and Earl all day. I wondered if maybe they had followed me to school and were hiding out in my class. They probably planned to jump out and embarrass me. My last class was a blur as I inspected every inch of the classroom from my desk.

I had barely grabbed my coat and backpack from my locker when Miss McCready, my third-grade teacher, called for our attention. "Before you go, class, I have a very important announcement."

The entire class groaned. Bad news was coming.

"We are having a very important language arts test first thing Friday morning." She pointed to the calendar.

"Noooooooooooo," the whole class moaned.

"Study everything in your notebooks from the last four weeks. You never know what might be on that test." She grinned.

No, she didn't grin. She smirked just like Aunt Crystal smirked when she gave me the towels. What was I in for now? How could I focus on studying when I had so much going on in my bathroom?

Eric, Deshaun, Chad, and I grabbed our gym bags and headed to the school gym for rep basketball practice. Eric kept poking me. "What's wrong with you? You don't look very good."

"Yeah," Chad chimed in. "We haven't really hung out since your party."

Deshaun nudged my shoulder. "You ditching your best friends?"

"No!" I answered all three questions at once. "I've got a lot on my mind right now." I couldn't tell them. They would think I was crazy. "Come on!" I took off on a sprint toward the gym. "Race you."

Hours later, I plopped myself down at the dinner table alone. "Coach Hawkins worked us like crazy tonight, Mom: warm-ups, power-dribbling, a half hour of full court press, a half hour of fast break, and thirty wind-sprints."

"I can tell." She wrinkled her nose. "If dinner wasn't ready right this moment, I would have insisted you take a shower first."

I cringed at the thought of another shower.

She slid a plate of food onto the table in front of me. "But I'll painfully endure your big-man smell while you eat. Then you can head right upstairs after supper for a hot shower."

"Okay." I shoveled a forkful of beef noodle bake into my mouth. "I have to study, too. We have a B-I-G language arts test on Friday."

After supper, I quietly slipped downstairs to Dad's office to see if I could figure out how to call Aunt Crystal on the computer like I saw Dad do with his clients. I moved the mouse. Each button asked me for a password when I clicked. I tried *Sweety*. That was his mushy name for Mom. Nope. Didn't work. I tried *Blue Bomber* because that was what he named the old Camaro in the garage. Nope. I tried his birthday. It was either 1938 or 1983, but I couldn't remember which. So I guessed. Nope. It wasn't 1938. And now I was locked out.

I tiptoed upstairs and headed to my bedroom, frustrated. Maybe that hot shower would help me think up another way to reach Aunt Crystal.

Chapter Seven

FULL OF BEEF NOODLE bake and language arts test nervousness, I prepared myself for anything **O** in the bathroom. I grabbed my orange towel and headed to the shower.

"Well, you're an easy one to figure out," I snapped the towel at the bathroom door. "You're obviously orange. I'm ready for you tonight. Give me your best shot." I stepped into the bathroom. Nothing. So far, so good.

Ziiiiiiiiiiiiiiiiiiiiiiip. I whipped back the shower curtain. Nothing. I exhaled. I couldn't do it. *It* was coming. I just knew it. Instead, I was going to outsmart this towel. I turned on the shower but didn't get in. The shower ran and I went to the sink. I splashed water on my pits, face, and hair, and toweled off as if I had my shower. I even dabbed on some of Dad's Zero-Cool deodorant. Then I turned off the shower and headed to my room.

"I'm a little disappointed that I could outsmart you so easily." I wrapped my towel around my neck. Maybe **O** was a dud?

Then I opened my bedroom door and my jaw dropped. A choir of overweight otters shucking oysters sang *Old MacDonald Had a Farm* at the top of their lungs. An old orthodontist accompanied them on an obtuse pipe organ.

"Shhhhhhh!" I pressed my hands over my ears and elbowed my bedroom door shut. My parents were downstairs and Taryn was in the bedroom down the hall. I didn't want them to know about the extreme chaos in my room.

An ornery officer, who wore a name badge that spelled *Orville*, and an ostentatious outlaw, oddly similar to the face on the **WANTED** poster that now hung on the wall, bounced on my bed. They shared a bowl of warm oatmeal and olives.

"Yuck!" I gulped.

The smell of hot oatmeal and olives stunk up my room. With one hand still pressed over my left ear, I pinched my nose with my right-hand fingers.

Oval Christmas ornaments dangled and swayed from the oscillating fan. An obscure group of owls perched on my curtain rod ate onions and spat the skins at my feet.

"No. No. No!" I kicked off the onion skins. This couldn't be happening.

Orange stripes and orchid flowers covered my comforter and curtains. "Ewwwww. Gross."

I gasped for a quick breath when an odd old octopus tapped me on the shoulder. He named all five oceans in alphabetic order. "Shhhhh," I hushed. "Shhhhhhh."

Oh no! I smelled my mother's opium perfume. Had she come upstairs or had someone in the room found her spray bottle?

"Out, out, out." I ordered everyone out through the window. "Octopus, orthodontist, outlaw, otters, officer, and owls, all out," I commanded in my loudest whisper.

An orang-utan wearing my dad's overcoat opened the window and helped everyone onto an oversized evacuation ramp. They slid down into the snow. I leaned over the ledge as they disappeared behind Mrs. Weeks's garage. "Phew!" I sucked in a huge breath of cool fresh air, but only for a millisecond. Mom's footsteps were just outside my door.

I dove toward the overflowing mounds of ornaments and olives scattered around my room and stuffed them into an oak ottoman.

My mom pushed open the door as I flopped on my bed in exhaustion. "Is everything all right, honey? It sounded like you had an orchestra warming up in here."

"Coach Hawkins worked us hard, Mom." It was the only thing I could think of to say.

"She must have. I think you need to hit the hay." She wrinkled her nose. "It smells in here. I think I better wash your dirty gym clothes." She bent over and picked up my gym bag. An olive rolled out of one of my gym socks. "I didn't know you liked olives." She winced with a puzzled look on her face.

"Good night, Mom." I was getting good at fake smiling.

"Good night, honey. Love you. I'm going to leave your door open a crack to help air your room out. Don't forget to close your window before you go to sleep." She nodded towards the window where all the **O** characters had just jumped out. I'm pretty sure the puzzled look on her face meant that she wondered why Dad's overcoat was in my room, but she didn't say anything. She just slipped out the door.

Earl and Ezra scampered out from under my bed after her. They pointed their hairy little trunks at me and giggled as they narrowly escaped the closing door. They were so rude.

I guess I really hadn't outsmarted the **O** towel tonight. I lifted the corner of the ottoman. The food and ornaments were all gone. I scratched my head. I plopped down on my bed and looked up to see that someone, most likely Ezra, had taped the little blue birthday card to my ceiling fan. *A, E, I, O, U, and sometimes Y.* "I really need to talk to Aunt Crystal."

Chapter Eight

I BLINKED IN A woozy, foggy, way-too-early-in-the-morning way. The first thing I saw was Mom's note on my Commander Hawk board.

Good morning, my eight-year-old ray of sunshine!

Ugh. I wanted to go back to being seven.

Your favorite maple bacon muffins are being served in the kitchen.

I loved my mother's maple bacon muffins. I wondered what the occasion was. She only baked them on special days. No other messages? That was weird. I dragged myself downstairs to the breakfast table and plopped my tired body on a chair.

"Good morning, Punkinhead." My mom smiled as she stood in front of the kitchen sink and wiped her hands on a dish towel. She peered out the window into our snowy yard.

I tried to pry my sleepy eyes open. "Morning, Mom." Then I noticed Taryn serving muffins to Chad, Eric, and Deshaun in the TV room. "Hey! What's going on?" I jumped up and headed toward the TV room.

"SNOW DAY!" Taryn announced. She charged into the kitchen and wrapped her arms around me. "And you get to play with me all day."

"Really? A snow day, Mom?" My fingers were crossed hoping the news was true.

"Yes." She nodded. "And the boys will be spending the day with us."

"We wondered when you were going to get up." Eric threw the couch pillow at me. "Two minutes more and we were bringing up some ice to wake you up in our own special way."

My three buddies laughed.

"Funny, guys." I flung the pillow back at Eric's head. "What do you want to do today?" I devoured one of my mother's amazing maple bacon muffins and wandered toward the recliner.

I spied Ezra and Earl as they snuck into the living room. Earl hoisted up the last piece of Deshaun's muffin with his trunk and set it on Ezra's back. They scurried under the couch. How come no one ever saw them but me? And Taryn saw them that one time.

"Hey, who stole my muffin?" Deshaun punched Chad in the shoulder.

"It wasn't me." He punched back.

For the next three hours, we played the best of seven Silver Cup hockey finals in our driveway - the Seattle Sting versus the Spokane Spitfires. Intermission included shoveling Mrs. Weeks's driveway and having a hot chocolate chugging contest. Then game seven of seven. The Sting won in overtime!

Taryn and Mom treated us to grilled cheese and bacon sandwiches to warm us up at lunch.

"Will you guys watch a movie with me this afternoon?" Taryn opened her eyes wider than I thought humanly possible.

"It'll cost you some of those snowflake sugar cookies that you and your mom baked this morning," Chad bargained.

She grinned from ear to ear. "You can have six." Taryn really liked Chad.

The five of us hunkered down with a plate of warm cookies in front of the TV to watch "The Waltz of the Snowflakes."

"Enough of this lovey-dovey stuff," Deshaun announced when the credits rolled. "It's time for the Snow Cyborgs to defeat the Polar Cyclops."

The guys and I built snow forts in the backyard and played out the snowball war of the century. The war ended as the four of us clutched our sides in laughter and gasped for breath. Chad had tripped over his own Polar Cyclops teammate, Eric, and face-planted in the snow.

"Let's surprise Taryn, and build a snow table and chairs for her," Chad suggested.

We constructed a H-U-G-E table and four chairs.

I snuck in the back door of the house and up to Taryn's room. I grabbed three of her stuffed animals and brought them outside. We set them up at the table and chairs and left a seat for Taryn.

"Hey, Taryn!" We opened the front door of the house and yelled. "Come outside."

Taryn peeked outside, then squealed, "Mom, look what they built for me!" Taryn put on her snowsuit and ran to join her stuffies at the table.

Mom brought out a second round of hot chocolate, but this time for the eight of us. "Boys, it's almost five and your parents want you home in a half hour. Please clean up the hockey gear and war zone. And remember, you have a basketball game after school tomorrow and a test on Friday."

"Oh yeah," we replied in unison.

"Unless we have another snow day." Eric crossed his fingers high in the air.

"Commander Hawk salute to go!" Deshaun announced.

We grabbed our hockey sticks (I mean lightsabers) and held them high. Clap, clap, clap. We smacked the blades together and chanted: "Faithful for keeps." Deshaun swung his lightsaber around in a circle low to the ground while we jumped over it. "Focus for life!" When we dropped our sticks, we did a four-way fist bump, swung around back to back, posed with hook-em-horn fingers, and roared: "And finish forevermore!"

And then the guys headed home.

That night, as Mom and Dad were glued to their favorite weekly TV show, I crept into their bedroom and grabbed Mom's phone. I wanted to video-chat with Aunt Crystal. I hoped she could help me out with this vowel towel mess.

I pushed all the buttons that looked familiar and suddenly, Mom's best friend, Rosie, appeared on the screen! I ducked so she couldn't see me and kept pushing buttons until the phone turned off. I threw the phone back into Mom's purse and ran to my room before Rosie called back! Yeesh, I just needed to talk to Aunt Crystal.

I lay on my bed and caught my breath. Then I hit the books again. "Focus, focus, focus." I pulled my notes closer to my face. I really needed to ace my test on Friday. I picked up my language arts workbook to study, but the little blue birthday card from Aunt Crystal fell out from between the pages. How did that get in there? **A, E, I, O, U,** *and sometimes* **Y**. Hmmmm.

But then my mind wandered. We needed to have more snow days.

Chapter Nine

I ROLLED OVER IN my bed and noticed that my Commander Hawk G-Brain watch hung on the corner of my dry-erase board. Mom must have been in to write on my board, 'cause I remembered that last night I dropped it . . .

"Oh no!"

I slept in!

No time for you, Commander Hawk! Sorry!

No time to shower!

My day was ruined!

Thankfully, the day turned out pretty super sick. After school, our rep team, the Briar Bobcats, pounced all over the Central Crossovers with a 34-19 win. Chad and Deshaun grew since last season and were massively amazing under the net.

As the point guard, I usually set up the post players to score, but tonight I netted eight points for the game. I still needed work at the line, but Coach Hawkins high-fived all of us and sent us to the showers.

Mom packed my gym bag that morning because I slept in. I grabbed the towel out of my bag and headed to the shower stall when I noticed she had packed my **U** towel. I skidded to a screeching stop. It felt like King Kong was beating on my chest.

Jonesy, one of our shooting guards, slammed into the back of me. "Hey, watch it."

"Sorry," I mumbled, and let him go into the closest shower stall. What if something happened with my **U** towel here in the locker room?

"Great game, Todd." Eric smacked me on my back as he ducked into the next stall.

"Yeah, thanks, Eric." I gulped, staring at the last remaining shower stall. I hung the ultramarine blue towel on the hook. I grabbed some soap and a bottle of shampoo from the pocket of my gym bag and noticed that the shampoo was called *Untangled*. It was super crazy scary that it started with the letter **U**.

The hot water made me relax a little. I squeezed the shampoo bottle, and the lid shot open like a champagne cork on New Year's Eve. The pop echoed like a cannon. Tiny unicorns spewed into the air like ten thousand mosquitoes. They lined the walls of the small stall. They marched with ukuleles. They marched with urns. They marched with umbrellas. They paused, only to poke me with their pointy umbrellas. Ouch. Little ouches all over. I squinted. They each wore a University of Utah t-shirt.

No, no, no. This can't happen.

Tiny pricks poked my head. I looked up. An unfriendly baseball umpire wore an un-tucked undershirt. He sat on top of the shower stall and spoke quietly in Urdu. He urged me with an upholstery needle to get out of the shower.

"Not a chance." I threw the bar of soap at him so he would go away. There was no way I was taking all this craziness into the change room for everyone to see!

I looked down at my chest and noticed a h-u-g-e tattoo of the flag of Uruguay. My mom would flip if she saw that!

I quickly shut off the water. I grabbed my towel from the hook outside the stall. I stuffed my uniform, now covered with Union Jacks, into my duffle bag. I threw on a shirt to hide the tattoo. As I buttoned up the shirt, I looked deep into an old, faded mirror that looked like it had hung on the door for fifty years. Whoa. A United States army unit commander stared back at me. I stared too because he had an ultra-pink bouffant up-do and stood on a set of uneven bars.

"Left, right, left, right, left," his gruff voice made me shudder. Thankfully, he uttered his demands in a low whisper.

I noticed the slight smell of urine. Yuck, was that the change room or the **U** towel taking things a bit too far?

I thought fast on my feet, grabbed the shampoo bottle, and squeezed out every ounce of shampoo. Then, I held it up really, really, really high in the stall and allowed the vacuum of the bottle to suck up every unwanted **U** item.

"Take that," I proclaimed in my strongest whisper ever.

A few remaining unicorns in U-boats dribbled between my toes and down the drain. Phew. I rubbed my stomach. I was sure I must have an ulcer.

I heard the team preparing to leave the locker room, so I checked the stall for any lingering **U** characters.

The coast was clear.

"Hey, Todd! I don't know what takes you so long, but get a move on." Deshaun stuck his head back through the change room door. "We're heading to your house for Ultimate Urban Pizza and pineapple upside-down cake. Your mom invited the whole team."

I stood utterly shocked.

I turned back for one last quick look around the dressing room. I spied Earl and Ezra lounging on top of the gym lockers. They rolled in laughter and pointed their hairy little trunks at me. They had watched the whole thing. One of these days, I was going to get them.

My dad met me in the hallway with a big high five. "I think you have a big **U** on your back."

My jaw dropped.

"You know, like a horseshoe. A good luck horseshoe. You sank almost every shot you made tonight. That's a great way to start the season."

"Thanks, Dad." I resisted the urge to feel for something stuck to my back.

Chapter Ten

NOT LONG AFTER THE team went home, I hit the books. But my eyes drooped like a sloppy, soggy piece of bread. I was space-cadet tired, but I had to study. Miss McCready said that this test was wickedly important. Ok. Maybe those were my words. But now that I was eight years old, I needed to show my parents that I could handle sports, school, and staying up late. Passing this test would be a good way to prove that. Of course, I still l had to work on my exaggeration problem, but that was minor compared to dealing with these towels.

I was just drifting off when my mom knocked softly at my bedroom door. "Honey, can we talk to you for a minute?"

A magnormous glob of fear shot through me. Had Mom and Dad noticed some of the strange things going on this week?

Did Rosie see me on the phone and tell Mom? Were they going to ground me for all the noise? Were they going to send me to a doctor? I really just needed to talk to Aunt Crystal.

"Ah, sure, Mom," I gulped. "Come on in." But it was Taryn with her, not Dad.

"Taryn has something she would like to say to you," Mom nudged Taryn in the back. "Don't you, Taryn?"

"Todd," Taryn bit her fingernails nervously. "Today I borrowed one of your birthday gifts without asking you, and I ruined it."

Immediately, I took a quick in-my-head inventory of my gifts.

"It was the towel that had the **Y** on it. I spilled some make-up from my Bobby-Jo Beauty set on my bedroom floor and I used your towel to clean it up. I didn't know that the makeup wouldn't come out. I'm sorry Todd. I can buy you a new one. And I can sew a **Y** on it for you."

I sighed in relief. "It's okay, Taryn. Aunt Crystal gave me six towels. I'm sure I can do with five."

I don't know who was most relieved: Taryn because I wasn't mad, my mom because I hadn't taken Taryn's head off, or me because I now had one less crazy vowel towel to worry about. That also meant that I wouldn't have to covertly try to get in touch with Aunt Crystal before she got home on Saturday. Phew.

As Mom and Taryn slipped out the door, my mom stopped and looked back at me with a smile. "You're really growing up, Todd. Thank you for handling this situation like you did. Don't study too long." She winked and quietly closed my bedroom door.

Oh, Mom. If you only knew.

I folded up my books and dropped them on my bedroom floor. I slipped under the covers and wondered what would have happened with the **Y** towel. I drifted off to sleep and tried to dream up my own vowel towel story. But I couldn't think of a single word that began with the vowel **Y**.

Chapter Eleven

"FAITHFUL FOR KEEPS, FOCUS for life, and finish forevermore." I saluted my Commander Hawk dry erase board as I rolled out of bed.

Happy Friday!

Great game last night!

Thank you again for forgiving Taryn about the towel.

One more day until Aunt Crystal got home and I could talk to her about those towels.

Do well on your test today.

Oh, Commander Hawk, I hope tests for eight-year-olds weren't as hard as it was being an eight-year-old. This has been a wacko week.

Keep working on your exaggerating.

No blunders this week. So far, so good.

I found your birthday card from Aunt Crystal stuck to one of last night's pizza boxes. It looked like it had dog hair on it, but I didn't want to throw it out in case you still wanted it.

Love, Mom!

Oh Mom, if you only knew that was elephant hair. And no, I didn't really want it anymore. I have had enough of **A, E, I, O, U,** *and sometimes* **Y**!

"I had the flat-out weirdest dream last night," I told the guys as we walked to school that morning. "I dreamed over and over and over and over again that Stevie Yzerman announced to the whole world on national TV that he loves Ypsilanti, Michigan. He wore his old hockey jersey and declared that he was moving to Ypsilanti to open the world's largest ice cream store called *Yzerman's Yce Cream Ymporium*. It was on every TV channel from one to 999. It was the biggest news of the day. Thousands of fans showed up. Some were really, really, really excited about the ice cream. Some complained about the spelling of ice cream and emporium with a **Y**. But most were just excited that he was moving to Ypsilanti. It was such a weird dream. And I must have dreamed it a kajilion times."

"Well, he'd be close enough to stop by and teach you some stick handling, because you stink at hockey." Chad laughed at his own joke and then took off in a sprint.

We all took off after him. Deshaun, Chad, Eric, and I slid into our desks just as the school bell rang.

Miss McCready welcomed everyone as she handed out the test.

"Class, take your time, focus, and think through each question." She dropped the rest of the tests on her desk and spun around. "I have a surprise that Principal Lemon has approved. If anyone can answer the bonus question correctly, your name will go into a draw for two tickets to the Premier showing of the movie, *Leap to Light-Speed: The Galaxy Awakens*."

"Woohoo!" The whole classroom exploded with full-blown fingers-in-the-mouth whistling. "Faithful for keeps, focus for life, and finish forevermore!" The entire class chanted Commander Hawk's charge.

"Now, turn over your paper and begin your test," she announced.

Language Arts Test

Name: _____

Date: _____

Question #1: List all six vowels in the alphabet.
Question #2: Write a verb that begins with each of the first five vowels.
Question #3: Write a noun that begins with each of the first five vowels.
Question #4: Write a proper noun that begins with each of the first five vowels.
Question #5: Write an adverb that begins with each of the first five vowels.
Question #6: Write a smell that begins with each of the first five vowels.
Question #7: Write a color that begins with each of the first five vowels.
Question #8: Write an adjective that begins with each of the first five vowels.
Bonus question: Write one word (any type) that begins with the sixth vowel, if you can!

I heard groans all over the classroom.

My shoulders relaxed. I smiled. I sighed. I had this one in the bag. It seemed like it was just moments later that I put down my pencil and put my head down on my desk.

"Todd, is everything Ok?" I heard Miss McCready ask.

I lifted my head, nodded, and smiled some more.

She made her way over to my desk. She grinned as she briefly glanced at my answers then bent close to whisper, "I see you studied well."

I smiled again.

I choked back a snicker as Earl and Ezra crawled onto Miss McCready's desk and disappeared into her briefcase. They gave me a big thumbs up, which is hard for elephants to do.

On Saturday morning, Aunt Crystal's 1957 lime green VW Beetle rumbled up our driveway. A-hunka-hunka-hunka. A-hunka-hunka-hunka, sputter, sputter, hisssss. I ran down the stairs, out the front door, through the snow, and jumped into Aunt Crystal's arms. "I didn't forget." I showed her my awesome test with the two movie tickets attached.

"**A, E, I, O, U**, *and sometimes* **Y**," we chanted together.

"And I chose to share my prize with you!"

As we walked up the stairs onto the porch, I saw Aunt Crystal smirk, but this time it wasn't at me. There were Ezra and Earl wrapped up neat as a bow inside the winter wreath on our front door.

Aunt Crystal looked down at me and winked. "Turning eight was a magical year for me, as well."

GLOSSARY

Amber – a color mixture between yellow and orange

Bouffant up-do - a type of hairstyle where the hair is pulled up on top of the head

Eggplant – a dark purple fruit; part of the potato and tomato family

Eucalyptus – an Australian tree/bush that produces a strong-smelling oil

Isla Fisher – a beautiful Australian actress

Indiana Jones – a fictional movie character that was an archeological professor that comes across many adventurous situations when searching for historical artifacts

Ivan the Terrible – was the Russian Prince of Moscow from 1533 to 1547, then the Tsar until 1584

Opium – juice from a poppy

Oscillating fan – an electric fan that stands in one place but swings side to side

Ostentatious – a person that acts in a way to be noticed

Shucking oysters – the term for opening an oyster

Stevie Yzerman – a retired professional hockey player and current general manager of a professional hockey team

U-boat – a German submarine used in WWI and WW2

Ulcer – an open sore on the inside of a person's body

Ultramarine blue – a rich bright blue color

Union Jack – the national flag of the United Kingdom

Urdu – the national language of Pakistan and one of the six national languages of India

Uruguayan flag – the national flag of Uruguay, a country in South America

Ypsilanti, Michigan – a city in the eastern part of Michigan with an approximate population of 20,000

Acknowledgments

It wasn't easy to *Grab Life by the Handlebars and Pedal Like Mad into this Wild and Wonderful World* of publishing.

But I had Stacey Weeks hoisting me onto the bike, Tara Ross steadying me from the handlebars, Heather Bootsma chanting praise from the sidelines, and Karen deBlieck pushing from behind.

You, my friends, have made this wonderful journey believable and a whole lot of fun!

I hope you see touches of your creativity throughout

Aunt Crystal & The Vowel Towels.

A special thank you to Adia. Your 7-year-old expertise finalized the details of this book.

Manufactured by Amazon.ca
Bolton, ON

33316813R00046